What Sort of Bird are You?

Tessa Foley is a poet whose work explores feminism, sexuality and the rejection of normalcy. Her debut poetry collection, 'Chalet Between Thick Ears' was published by Live Canon in November 2018 and has inspired a series of Live Canon films. The same year, Tessa also self-published 'Garden', illustrated by her sister, Anna Foley, to raise money for the Portsmouth Abuse and Rape Counselling Service where she volunteered for three years. She has recently been recognised in the Ware Poets Competition, the Charroux Poetry Prize and the Canterbury Literary Festival Poet of the Year Competition.

First Published in 2021

by Live Canon Poetry Ltd
www.livecanon.co.uk

© Tessa Foley 2021

978-1-909703-51-3

A CIP catalogue record for this book is available from the British Library.

Cover illustrations: Anna Foley

Acknowledgments

Earlier versions of these poems were previously published in the following publications:

'It's not me, It's you', *The American Journal of Poetry*, August 2018
'Postcards from my Father', *Live Canon Competition Anthology,* 2017
'Hospital Living', *Fredericksburg Literary Art Review*, Spring/ Summer 2016
'Why Not?, *Atrium Poetry,* September 2020
'American Dream', *Spillwords*, May 2016
'Real Monsters', *Poets Versus Sexual Harassment: An Anthology*, May 2020

'The Forever Children' was commended in the Ware Poets Open Poetry Competition, July 2020

'In Case it Comes Back' was shortlisted for the Canterbury Literary Festival Poet of the Year, September 2020

Contents

Old Bird

Mean Bird

New Bird

*For Junior
and the Warm Corner*

Old Bird

My Birthday

Wall on fire. Of all things I resist I
consist of an eye and a crocodile tail,
swoop up and a spiral and sigh of relief.
I'm intended and meant
            to be on the day
that they choose.

A choice ensues for the life in the distance
hazy and smoke-filled. Trust me I'm new,
all know-how in fists on my pie of a head
flattened and cushioned
            in revelling pups. I've
got no protection

I'll be out on my ear and it's coming, I'm coming!
and all that I hear in my deep velvet wood
is nicety nice I'm a girl so I love it,
push it and shove it
            and thar she blows,
and that's my nose! I am

carnival mirror I'm Churchill in white,
oh so many touches, a much of a muchness,
I'm one of a hundred in matching tin hats. We're
elephant chains,
            painstaking detail
of dots and figures

and as I get bigger, I'm less and less them,
I'm going to be flower and concrete tree,
mammoth and dancer and ragged of breath
I'll be outer reaches with daggers on chains
I'll never explain,
            they lost me before
I was born.

Sky and Sea

They shattered, they split and they left two,
The sky, the sea – a me and a you.

The sky and sea hate all the wind and wet,
But never forget one blue afternoon,
Or tunes all sung in many voices,

So much for sky and sea to do,
But only through the tides and moon,

And all the bruises of the blue, the me and you
Are still just that,
The sky and sea, not scorched, not drained.

Goes on the rain,
Goes on the wave.

They threw the bolts of weather and left two,
The sky and the sea is me and you.

All their Affair

Monday to Saturday, it's fattening, flattening,
a whisky away from a big unsaid fight.
Straight from the glass, not daring to ask
what you did when you weren't here last night.
I was garden ornament, I was birdbath.
Light from front windows licking the path.
I never said nothing, I never asked who
and you? you were zipped, clipped in your voice
that never leaks, cracks or spills, dignity
bound, you might not make a sound
from four-thirty to five in the morning. So cold
in the searing dawn sun knuckling over
the sill and in to the bed that I let you
creep in to. A red raw balloon
swelling in my chest with all the best insults
all saved up for you. You sit as a child
in an Anderson shelter, not knowing what you'll lose
when it all starts blowing. The best days have died,
scattered wide and to winds, never begins,
never ends, just is. We're nothing and everything
all needled together, I never said "Forever"
I never said nothing.

Simple Arithmetic

She took the peach for a teacher
and made it a sum
she could do *Me plus a luxury equals*
your love and it stayed as her way when she found him

dawdling in
from the shore to a pier
it was as though they'd met moon tides and laugh lines
somewhere before, when they had played

knockdown ginger
at completely wrong doors
sat facing each other
unseen in a train's
certain carriage

and when the steam vanished
from the pane in between

unmarriage they went for
at the pace that a spaniel makes
into the sea, her underslip merely
a costume
for her calculate dip
outreaching a hand for her balance he asked:
shingle? *it's desperate, hard on the sole*
and she ducked below surface
blue goes her life

Make me your wife she said as she laid
on the beach but she didn't
quite mean it and she was
holding a peach.

Raising Philippa

They left her, they did,
in a fridge with the light on

a whiteness upon her,
she ate all her own skins,

no worse off than someone,
no better than mud,

denied till one man
one day at a window

knew she was real.
She heard each of the sighs

through the willow-herb close,
plastered to face

with no railing to hand,
she wobbled and fell

to her death on occasion,
no relation to nurture,

she was the pondlife
that sat by the pond

and was seen. They left her,
with a coat peg unhung

she wore jumpers in summer
and shorts in the rain,

pre-slaughtered, slapped
and despised in the eyes

of the builders. They won.
They'd designed and destroyed

till she sat on the bench.
She broke her own neck

when she'd grown, to be noticed,
she raked over the soil

on which she was taunted,
unwanted she walked

every breath a regret,
blown up camel's hump,

she sat and was watered,
a seed that turns nova

in one little week. Future
days all unwrapped

once she knew she was real,
not a turn for the neighbours

whose warm-up act
cooled down. When he told her

he'd seen her, someone
heard the first scream,

and she stood, tulip-bordered
with her face to the birds.

Monster in the Trees

As old as me,
as wide and still as the December
I was born,
the monster in the trees.

He's up to his knees
in breeze block and snow.
I face where he stands, eyes
brimming over leaves.

He can't come to me,
but we go walking, slurp
thud in cement and I worry for his cold
feet in my dream

behind my wall sleep he's
the concrete part of me.
Knock knock in the Keynes
his spikes they come in threes

the monster in the trees.

Boyland

He is bleached
when they smack the light switch
and there's no plastic point
to be laughing or crying

because home
is a sea with a giant, fat
gap instead of an end to the line
he goes blue telling lies

aubergines on his side
in the pork of the cloakroom.
Noticed by nothing
but furthersome fists,

his voice is a small
yellow bone, an unwanted
knapsack, they trap him
in bike baskets.

They pedal permissives,
with him on the edge,
he is the fruit they hang
over the cliff

his thread wrists unpickled
by mother and friend,
they leave him, sleepless
with no one to call.

He's a seed in the dark,
under flowerbed. Folks,
his boyland is mouthless,
no parks, no parades

until loud, slurring
grown-ups break quiet
off in chunks.

Postcards from my Father

My Daddy, he left me there under a tree,
to grow up in the dapple with the fruit to break teeth in
alone in the crib.

I rattled like mad so he'd hear a pure bell,
buy and sell, off he swept, up in the branches
and into the sky.

But I must confess, he sends postcards and I
I have a teddy from each fifth of the world
and I shoot an inch taller

waiting for mail. By myself, I have found
a yellowish trail, squirming away from each
passing touch.

I am so much discovered by grown ups, I find.
With my spine in a brace, facing forward forever, not
hearing a sound

they give me notice, like Daddy who left
without tears but rolling Keep Left signs
aflame in his eyes.

Whilst he trips to the moon, I'm marooned in the red,
my plot is too buried, down under the gum tree,
disease in the roots,

I jack up my boots and go hiking in mud
where my name has been questioned and
stamped in and spread.

Feeling dead, hearing birds chant in branches above
my cold crown, I am down, I am paid in pink sweeties
to hush on my lips

and staring at drips, on back windscreens to count out
the secs, stone-handed, felled wrists 'round their shoulders,
I am the shallowest

notch on the post. I just watch as my postcards
thumb by, each tiny hitchhike, a view
with a click that's not

the latch on my door. They adore me, they say
and I can only believe, don't make like the gum tree, don't
leave. They don't leave.

I love you too, Clarkey

I cried, she said
when Daphne died,
Daphne who?

Although
I thought I knew just
who she meant.

Daphne, you know,
she was married to Des,
yes, she was my favourite.

Your favourite?
Really?
Not Lenny? Not Henry?

No. Daphne, I loved her,
she was the best,
Des thought so too,

Lizzie said, as I drew
an eye on my rough book.
Look, I said,

Daphne? How could she
be best? What else
did she do?

'Cept for the
'I love you too'
she was cool, Lizzie said

and that was the end,
then when Lizzie was gone,
The weight that I knew

she loved Daphne
was great,
so I had to tell you.

Bad Things

What I learnt in amongst all the brambles and headgear,
reliable shoutings from the woman next door,
in between all the films
about men with ambitions/whips and the songs by the girls
in the leathery skirts I'd take words 'bout the birds
and see through the gaps.

Fell out of three trees at a time into a
pile of cracked ice cream sauce, I'd learn how
to turn off a light
when I left a wide room and then run without breath
from the face I'd see screaming, discover each time
this was not a bad thing.

In the midst, I'd take vice or advice from the speakers,
get how to clean vinyl on a velvety bum note,
there it is, there's no rhyme
and that woman can't sing, there it is – The Bad Thing –
the bad thing in the tune but when the music is flat
you can see the sun set.

Hear how big ears made him look like the FA Cup,
how I'd only fall down if I danced in a pit,
in the middle of voices
my choices weren't beans. Said the queens to my face,
Oh you'll never be Charming, but the garden don't stop
just because there's a fence.

I learned bad things were the biggest, the best
and the sky, till one New Year in the shower,
one single chime, one year short
of forty, my mind said not the worst thing
will be most important. Not all bad things
are important at all.

Greenfinch

My worry was
a head shaped like an onion
in the mirror, lips for kissing fish,
when love for my first one
crawled up my leg.

He wasn't a singing boy
and his skin was crass with every bristle,
washed up and bleeding
dry on a hook,
he blew away all dragging manly men.

It was pencilled heart
in chemistry textbook,
shirt stuck to my arms, a long
wait through the window
to the walking dog and growing grass.

Night time cooling open slats
clouted my fat hands
on clenching sheets and I was parked
in my blazer, furry hot in the morning
waiting for the bus.

Unsalted probes from all
the girlish frontish-row, they
wanted to know,
haughty whispers dropped on gym mats,
I couldn't tell them all I felt was cold.

Lilac at the Back Door

In my bed, I call out that I miss the flowers,
only a shorticle nightie away
from my truest guess who climbed up into honeymoon,
pressed his guns against someone else's
Friday breads. Now in this fence off,
this seventies sit-come home street,
all the grey grouts, the gaps crumbling, the dry,
my hostage and I would like to announce
that we linger no more under wisteria.

In my sleep, I call out that I miss the flowers,
no dotty white leaves nail my crest to a bench,
this is the set of the clock that I know
when I'm broken, this is the day I decide
I can't breathe. The bottles all sing
when they rub skins under plastic, like every day
was the dentist, they snap that I swallowed their Zmas,
defaced by the carpet, I am bought off by proof,
this is the Winter I was cracked in the bar.

Out of my window, I yell for my flowers
through iodine bruises and fried opinions
in woks, all lilac-frocked priests are the petals,
the peonies, even when it's my birthday
they blow out the match. So I shattered and spat
at my princes, I shot them all down with a well-chosen
juke. Hullo, my dear friend, I am desperate
to peel so look, come and get me
and my ventricle slow.

In my own box I give up the flowers,
this is a fat 'Why' I'm trapped underneath,
the day the Earth's goodwill snapped and handed out
bites from a glass and a screw
and a driver.

Old Girls Lost

My children live in 1993, 4, 5,
they have little school probs,
their jobs are in Summer
with uniform, badge, and I live today
with children who give me
worries, in stories
they told me twenty years ago or more,
I'm floored by teacher,
trouble with a woollen tucked
right 'round the waist.

These are my children,
live in 93,
94, 95, they are all alive,
not a one died, they live, they survive
for Friday night when The Word
with Terry Christian
shows 'em all about life, I concern myself
with children that are no childs anymore.

Outside my door
is Scared Spice,
she lives with love
for a choirboy who didn't
quite look twice.

And sleeping over
is Loud Mouth Type
who answers back to Mrs Wife. My life
did not get older
and I am not in life.

For children didn't grow inside,
they'd-a built a house within my eyes
before I'd even bled.
And made me blind to other kids
the ones that wouldn't be.

My children live in 93, 4, 5,
And there I spike with little likes,
dislikes for minor keys,
the trees are saplings for my life despite
the leaves that fall off overnight.

My children's kids are not in 95,
not 93 or 94 and nothing matters more
than them, their floating spores
are real and not a class 4
recall.

Giggling behind a door, in 1994,
in uniform, my poor, bright children,
all adored
as if I were the mother,
gathered up a snood with all the
school days curled inside.

They left behind their cold, green books,
went Bride, some twice, one died.

As tall and swaying adult souls
they left behind
the hot fried lab coat times,
and I —

I'm on their side like six thousand nights
have never gone, the kids,
we all eat opal fruits
at scratched desks in the sun.

Gwendoline

I thought the flowers in your garden were ghosts,
pale bloated ballerinas that strung along the seasons
and I cried when they decreased in my fist,
all the bliss of the barefeet on the baked mosaic
melted in scraps of pulpish pink.

They told me a greenhouse was parked on previous years,
I begged to know how it looked, how hot did it
feel in the fifties? All the slanted years since
shook to my birth, the little brides in a chain
as I counted the petals.

It was taken away but I can see you in your garden,
grab at the air where you should have been standing
catching the wish of hairspray unbottled,
your silk on stone hands with the neighbour's cat.
I'm only small when I think of you,

sun lights the cloud as it folds itself behind,
I heard you on the stairs a year after you were gone,
but I knew it was you. Not a ghost, just a guess
at the dust in the earth, the overtly pale
soil in the garden where the snowdrops always grow.

Shoot for the Mooncup

Over China teacups, here's my sweet jelly
toast to the most
popular sex organs this planet has known —
for Millicent, Maud, I'm applauding the grown
and still going strong, I flew via Kent
to this ovule-nation, and to Bartholin cyst y'all
listen to this —

my cyclical sisters I've got previous on this,
since 11 I've insisted
on bleeding heart liberally and tendering breasts
and the rest? I hear sneers that I bleed without dying
oh I dye it alright and I dye it all red,
in my head it's no different, downstairs it's a riot —
metres and metres

of endometriosis, my fibroids
devoid of socialness
awks. So I'll talk and declare I'm foof loose —
fanny freely, I'm really a miracle of ancient
invention, conventions are bollox, you don't need to
explain, sometimes pain, sometimes weight gain
pelvic flawless, you know…

Cervix with a smile, a fantastic elastic
balloon from the moon —
the pin up has periods, in her pretty polycistics,
though Grable may not have felt able to table
a fable about labial song, progression
comes on — and I'm on! I'll be on until Thursday
and then when it's later

come Katy Perry Menopausal, or Lactatum
O'Neal, we could be
real & not ashamed of the wheel, so spill!
and santé to the Uber, the uterus, a stand
to be taken when they ask at the till, "Would you like a bag?"
"No my good man, I'll hold tampons like swords"
cause I can't be ashamed

of a natural refurb. Unperturbed
I will carry them naked
in hand, stand ragging them soft at bus stops
and brunch. I am bursting with issues, I'm leading
scar tissue, not pining for lining as it falls
down the bend. Send me to the scout hut where I'm
sorry for blood?

You're a fud, you're a bonehead
if you think it's shame,
watch the dame, the professor, the creator, the bleed,
all we need is your silence, so shut it indeed,
and watch me, football solar plexus,
the nexus of life, no sexus, no sexus!
Watch me. Period.

Not Coming Home

Bannister, she's not coming home,
all your woody article, your slip-slide to the floor,
she won't sticky finger,
she won't spot iron tears through pork fingers again,
she's not coming home, pass it on.

Back door, she's not pushing through anymore,
your sill with the broad bean, your unpompous click,
she's not going to pea-brainly nut you again,
her paws on the jamb,
she's not coming home, pass it on.

Warm Corner, she's not sitting in you again,
she's got weddings to trash, there's cava to schlep,
her elbows won't burn on your surrogate fluttering,
ribs have all crackled up and gone to the south,
she's not coming home, pass it on.

Landing window, she'll never be here, not at all,
your concorde silver arm and perfect punched holes,
she'll not overwater a cyclamen burst and she won't
try and lean out to see in the pellets,
she's not coming home, pass it on.

Garden path, she won't take you, not ever again,
her own sand matching yours as she combed,
back and forth, she'll not crush the mint and stand
with her face on the gate, smelling heatstroke and rust,
she's not coming home, pass it on.

Mean Bird

Shall I Kiss Her?

It's not flamingo weather
not today in Covent Garden,
fortnightly taxi's axis
on the wet skidaddle street,
and it's sweeter than a doughnut
to watch her walk ahead.

She is waist and chest and shoulders
above the rest, when she shares her change —
one finger on a fifty-pence —
thin splashes round her ankles
and a darting, birding, blinding eye
I'd dye the thought to red of
shall I kiss her?

A warning from the future,
her unparted hair
in walls before the market,
where even pigeons think she's sexy,
in the next dream I have
I'll be her coat worn against her
on the bridge, across a clawing night.

I Built my own Church

I built my own church today.
The name on the door is
He who is called He is but we all know who made it
so fingertip genteel and stitched lacy detail,
on to the green slaps of county downs.
Just in case they didn't know,
I'd pointed directly to Heaven.
Me, Sir, me! I got it right.

To make it quite simple, my rod shoots to divine,
and under my roof you can cool down in August,
I've done all the standards, but better of course,
I make threats in glass,
in sticky green lessons
in lellogram leaves and the Knights die in sections
but it's for the leaseholder so all a good cause.

On my aspired spire there are forty-nine crows
and they're under nothing, on top of creation,
not one illusion of who is the king,
but the men lay face down
between sinewy toes, soaking up centuries
of the begging before them,
the pleas for no snow
and for daughters to bear.

Touch the wall under Mary
and you're touching my hand,
where I stood and I cried
in your place on a whole
host of Sundays and you realise one day
that He'll be exchanged, the milk-teeth white man
taking his bow on His last lengthy night,
in His place will be mirrors
and stained glasses in rows,
but my name is engraved on each eighteenth stone
and my hand will touch yours
in your blankest moment.

All Fall Down

My book was taken from me
when I'd only just learned to read,
the front page only mostly,

I crossed myself at the gates and went on in,
alone, to read the braille
along the railings 'round the goldfish,

I fell into direction
but the echoes were so loud,
that I had to break the patterned path
and so I found yourself beneath the hornbeam
looking left and righteous.

Thought I'd ask you several questions,
not one I imagine you'd answer,
I'd always wanted to know just why
the worst you ever looked
was when we met,

my writing hand left unforgotten
bones of how on one wet bench,
your face ran with the rain but, since,
your eyes have turned to all the colours
of a winter party.

On kitchen tables I had planned my life,
and worked a finger 'round in circles,
there was you,
crossed out and written in again.

When they asked me why you'd never been deleted,
I would hide beneath the mattress
with a headbutt to the floor

I'd make it out that I was sat
where they keep the waves before they use them,
or with you, hating every second.

They asked me where I was before
and I told them… Oh nowhere,
I've just been in Victoria Park
watching the terrapins blink,

and it was truth of sorts,
I'd caught a virus that made me fall down in the leaves,
though piles of Autumn had amassed
I hurt myself
was barely clothed

and was hating you dearly
for never quite being there,
then hating me
for being where you'd asked.

I didn't marry him for him
or even hymns,
or bright pink aisles,
I walked for miles toward the man I'd never like
for you to watch me go

just in case you lived with my face
on the tip of your tongue

and there I honeymooned in cafe lights,
one RSVP in my pocket.

I dropped my hand to where your name was written,
and it felt like kissing you.

Hospital Living

I want my shoes back, pointy-toed scarlet,
to dance on mosaics, I want to stand up
without a draft slivered to the bottom of top,
my eye worn from drawing on a stranger at dawn.

My name is not cut up in sections these days,
in full it's blue smudged on the wall with a star,
sometimes red underline.
This could be my time.

I'm easy chair charming, a dent in the mattress,
that's a print to be found, a magnificent actress,
you know you can swallow, encore, Oh No! Spit!
and they own my remains, fact they own my todays,
in their witchly smooth claws.

I want to play ball on a lawn in my past.
My heart has a plan. My sheets aren't my own, I'm a
space in the line-up, billed
beneath conducting hands,
my parts high-strung puppets and inner arm scratched
with silky milk serving, it froze me in time,
snuck me past the back door
but my slowing will begs
to taste one more bottle of red, I'm not dead.

And I sink in a spiral and hear crying horses,
see through a mist, pour myself over ledges,
folding and spooling, I'm cake mix, a soup
tied in suture, their stitched Campbell container,
my fingers as wings not twitching or light,
I'm so flat but the world is at risk from my side,
I giggle in veins and whiten my eyeballs
this means I still breathe.

It's flickering tea time, my tongue is so present,
just sip it, they say. My execution was poor
so I've stayed for a day, maybe more, they don't know
so whilst clinging, I want. I want church bells and cookies,
ten more trips to the bookies, team songs
on the beach and then sex on a gurney, a lover
to burn me, it don't
stop till it stops.

Why Not?

Why not be your biro?
And be held between your dryish fingers
on a Tuesday, on the train,
when you do your quickest thoughts
over clues in black and white,
be rattled on your teeth,
sit on your diary, on your desk and
wait for you to use me.

Why not be your fancy shirt?
And be fluttering against your chest expensively
when you are feeling great at dinner
till you spill black, vein wine on my stitches,
and swipe at me but leave a mark,
be thrown into the dark, hanging
till you're too fat
to take me out.

Why not be your holiday?
The space that you lie down in,
be the time that you exhale on windows
with pretty scenes beyond,
when everything goes fast and messy,
be the place you laugh and sleep the most,
or the place you wish you hadn't come,
the plane you missed to Gatwick.

Why not be your wedding ring?
Slide up and off your hand
when it's time to soap the bowls,
call out in a cinema when the movie light
bounces off you and your popcorn, be dumped
off the bridge over the creek
and dwindle to the silt when you can't
stand the sight of me.

Why not be your sorry?
The thing that appears when you are weak
and tired and when your skin is bad,
the thing you feel deep in your lap
but can't quite put your lips to,
I'd make you a torch of embarrassment
and strap you to a lifetime
of looking like a fool.

The Boy from the Orphanage

Infected and sweetly directed at mother,
the woman of so bulbous a tone
she left home and a boy
to be fractured, compacted
and wrapped, hard-boiled,
wait a week, wait a week
you pain in the arthouse.
One day, he would be
untrue on a tree,
lynched from the stars.
Sister Abigail's party
entreated to come
he vanished from the Avenue,
closed down in the Close,
a finch stopped his tweets
a rose sneezed at the flowers,
he lay still for hours,
what a rush to be living
when you know how it ends.
What a scene. He tried hard
to be headed for deadness,
and then he was gone,
the car, far too far over
the cliff, rich and hard,
all confessions were whistled,
no faith left in Adam
as he dropped past the door,
just past four with a foregone
conclusion and never
a minute's desire
to be news. His gallant
and hallowed mistake,
a piss-taken, Snap!
and his traces are gone,
he's a fiend of the Earth,

pursed lips 'round the pit,
tipped into percentages,
all those tries
were now leagues tied up
under the drop,
after one knock
or two on the wood
from inside, he cried
at the life, it wasn't
his life he was given.

Suburban Cuckoo Selected

Mummy owns a shelf that she puts me on
with boys she likes.

She closes up the cardboard box,
spills in mint balls through the cracks

walks away
to leave me to explain my frozen natural assets.

She tightens up the straps around my band
and gives me oats to vomit back,

the bridal tack, the bit in my teeth,
gives the boys a half crown each.

Mummy owns a sporty car
and lets them all have rides,

She invites them to the royal box,
it's the worms she loves the best,

the slimiest and she's happy-ness,
the ones who tell her we could be sisters,

who want it served in silver swigs,
thought beyond their teeny reach,

no matter if the town is red with blood
of all of the women he hated before,

Mummy puts my hand in his, my dress is black
and purple on the inner seams,

he and mummy polka on the biggest day,
they have their day again again.

And I stay within corset and smile prison bars,
they dance and pick maps till one of us drops.

American Dream

I was missing for weeks when I realised
I'd slept through it all.
How far deep in to sleep I was willing
to go, to discover the new,

a country of seats by the window, my loves
could grow old without my watch stopping time,
in my leagues of unwoven inputted lines
I'd discovered America as explorers had not.

It smelt as I knew, like petrol and biscuits,
on the orange hillsides I wheeled on two tyres
with my pounds all forgotten, in right and left states
to the middle and up. This place like a cup

or a womb on the atlas,
I traced my cold finger from fallopian down,
each town with a story,
my future curled up in the best of the west.

In motels in distance I was different straight after
I'd washed face and hair in American soap,
I'd needed fresh hair and my shirt tails were audibly
clapping my leave,

scarecrows lined up in ranks as I drove,
not one waved hello, but they all knew my path
as I drove coast to coast
from one lipless shore to another.

I knew I'd be frank here and do it my way,
under gigantic trees, I could even be
scarlet, the confident Miss in magnolia
skin, who'd not walk on the side, elevate

or die trying. Collect calls like stamps, and at home
I was tired, grey canvas licking
forty old wounds, in this cooked yellow air,
I could be any movie or song that I'd choose.

I'd heard "Be afraid" but I stood like a brave,
beaming up at tart lights on the tips of the towers
as cold England intoned on my own FM wave
"No one visits this place to be unimpressed,

everyone wants to leave changed or to stay."
And I'd stay, Maine in May,
Oregon for the good. When I woke
it was over, so with sobering tear

I admitted my states
were of mind and on loan,
my York was not new and my pants were not under,
the wonder of west were sleep candy alone.

The Forever Children

There, as a Q in one unchanging font,
as they jack in the diamonds, the friskiness pills,
she's still ring-a-rosencrantz, dancing the floor.

The elk in the room is her age as it wanders
and steps two at a time to its hospital bed.

She thinks that she hears one third of him call
but stays dancer and torn tin, dressed to depress
with all the beams from the ball.

Then there's that song that starts like a snake
then folds schadenfreude

into a brimming brag sou'wester grin,
she was always king, with a kiss and no kids,
she was always a dancer for them,
in a ring.

She did everything early except growing up,
she masters the fingering: Brighton and bones.

There for the door, the trailers, the blabs,
shadowed, white teeth and not once is a filling
'less you count the fussless she met every night
taking tights down one leg at a time,
fingernails falling down into the bowl,

she's not chose to be still,
her frightening dance,
still doing trivial, meaningless meat,

swallow,
infect,
and not be dead yet,
reject rings,

bat back seedlings,
wise as a lark —

it started and ended with her in the bath
looking back up to a window,
that's relative,
meanly the size of her unadorned hand.

And seeing the bet that she made with herself
— I can outlast the others —
and she made it, as planned.

Engage Me

Swell — I'll put your name down
in my little white book,
then
when we have the cash,
I'll spray your mother fuchsia fantastic,
a drastic becoloured,
and in drag, we'll get married,
Then pop-a-cap-a-nisi
the minute we clink.

I won't drink to this union
because it's a wretch,
a bouquet of vetch and then
catch!
Pansy bean faces that peer from the basket,
I will not spend my Sundays
buying shoes with this no one,
I won't sit behind countryside tractors for fun.

But oh meo become,
it's eighteen years hence,
a fan of the fence, I swing to their breeze,
Polish cheese, parboil socks,
had the locks changed,
and my door's burgled fleece,
one piece at a time, they chip you with rings,
all the things fairytale
are a tethering bore.

Idolatry

They could always smell the night ahead on her
even from her corner,
Laura's shallow in shadows
but *they* watched
on the left side of worship

whilst the Pauls and the Johns lined up,
in inches, backs to the terrace,
the Sinema Queue
for her doublish features and
no break in the middle.

She was a beaming S
with footfalls up nightclub stairs,
they all stopped to look.

The jeans and the lips,
snaking tips on the make up,
she cast in a scarf ten metres long,
making fans think Isadora and axles,
the black on the blonde.
Laura's public grew warm.

Blue and wet on their haunches,
taunted blush by her syrup,
her fizzing scotch bonnets
dropped into each drink.

Where they could be foils
she was the fencer,
caked up to the lashes,
she was each drop in the clouds.

They wanted it all from
the day she first screamed
to the night she last yawned.

From her ovaries twisted
to her bald braking light
uphill and downmarket

her ancestral star and its hole in her stone,
the tome of her diary
placed into their hands.

Their grudge,
their great love,
their endless absorption,

from the draughts on the peaks
to the wrecks on the beds
they swear there'll be no one's possession like hers.

They hoped there'd be space for them
now in the light,
a lead role audition,

they're chief sobbers and grabbers
but the world still wants her.

So wearing her shirt
they wave hankies
two thousand tears heavy
as her pieces dismiss,

that life in one box, all locked up
— a present for God.

The dimmer switch flickered worldwide
and she went,
now they'll sluice
into glass slippers too small
for green eyes.

Pantomime Daddy

Wears the stripey black trews with news on every cufflink,
can tell a story to adore me, and he can tell a tale
with a whale and a mouse, in his curlicued house
I'd be safe. I'd have to be good, spit polish the wood,
split chess pieces in time, on the lime green bed,
grinning with guess, he's the best he will tell me,
better than boys, all the toys that they play with
don't tussle with me, he's a cartoon of daddy,
he sings all the right tunes, all the men in the moons
        and the dishes with spoons.

He is warm, he is nightly, he is old but he's sprightly,
can be trusted to put up the tree, and three weeks later
he'll dust down the baubles, twine up the lights,
we can't get into fights, he gives me an orange and
peels off one skin, calm water in the cradling eyes,
he gives me my gloves and then points at the skies,
if you can see fireworks, my girl, then you're a star,
a far away building is castle, is king,
the thing that he gives me is nothing I knew
        I grew only in bones.

When he phones, he is only a minute away,
not a postcard from Biscay, a letter from school,
all the rules that were missing are now there in the kissing,
firm guidance at hand, I am MJ, less mad,
Rita Pan in a nightdress and I never got old,
he told me my bedtime and vosened my hair,
there is a fence and a path and roof with a stack, like
back in the drawings I made when I wished,
and they dished me no prizes, his wisest and greyness
he walks me to bed, and instead of a goose
        I've a kiss on the forehead.

Blighty

An inflatABLE girl
she was up and down with the seasons,
the darkness crammed into her bloom of a mouth,
she said she was so pleased to see him
and meant it while standing on the lip of the alley
where he'd waited to find her,
his blood walked in ice
around his thin limbs
he proposed that a ring
was what he would give her
and it bored her to hear the phone
time and again,
the signpost he was,
pointing aloft to the peaks and the troughs
all over abroad,
a life measured in air miles and packets of salt,
the balm before the great storm,
he was linseed rubbed in
to her tight whiteish shoulders,
he crooned he would take her all over the world
in pocket diary form,
she'd be with him but
never herself see Japanese waves
touched by the branch of a fingering tree.
It wasn't the bells rung,
but rung of a ladder,
a step to an adult,
to gaze down where she'd say —
she was so pleased to see him
and mean it,
but love, it was weedy and frail on the wall
where she pressed to his keepsakes,
felt loved as the young.

Dearest

The moment I killed her, she drifted into focus
and I could see the world as it was surely meant,
unpainted and abandoned, a derelict place with beams
and struts that creak beneath the weight of human pulse.

She had always made me angry, blocking out the warmth,
she took my tiny hands in winter, made them colder,
and stalked in to each boldly-coloured room, orders flying
bullet-hearted and with rigid hair, unmoved.

She pointed upwards to the moon's thin slice of birth,
she read the book of myths for set ten minutes every night
and lifted corners of her mouth without smiling,
she told me in the way she walked that I should not be here.

I was bathed in TCP and connected to the TV set,
to Munsters, Shake'n'Vac ads and had a crunchy duvet
that made me cold when I was underneath and then made me
decide that her old bony soul would stop a clock.

The moment I killed her I loved her in a way
that she had never known and when her eyes blinked out
I think she felt a daughter's faithful puncture, understanding
it was all I could do to make a difference in her heart.

Conditions of Friendship

Know the code,
my finger prod when Mr Vale says 'box',
colour Marley's girlfriend's teeth
in your brother's framed class photo,
answer the phone by singing 'Saught and Pepa' here,
don't ever tell my mum.

Press the bell in queer morse code,
don't die,
ignore wet rot in family kitchen,
say my best film's utter shite,
don't buy the shirt I want but can't afford,
stand around like a prick while I wait for my bus,
and always tell me the girl I love
looks like a mole.

Join me on the rounders pitch
at the back, for a fag,
fall through alarmed doors in nightclub,
try and sell me while I sleep,
tell me my new bins are shite,
best my pool arm,
break my heart,
plan my life with you and me in mansions
and a soft top
and a permanent Tudor costume,
stay up all night
just talking about one song.

Frighten me with smells,
make up words,
take photos of me while I sleep, learn my weaknesses,
exploit them, tell me
my whole life's been shite,
explain the Lucy sex noise,
be forgiven, be the end,
don't die,
don't ever tell my wife.

This is the Big Life and You Don't Have to Have it

An adult is something
I never wanted to be. To be
grown up is to be feeling bad
and saying to someone littler
it's you, you're why
my bad mood's bad.

It's walking
out of a room, no matter
who's still in it. And
slapping switch to black, it's taking
time for nothing except growing
a small person's

smallness. It's holding
hostage grubby hands
and educating looks
to see the danger or the difference
and rinsing out the magic
from a pair of tiny eyes, it's

painting skies with forecast clouds,
it's sneering at the dreams, it's thinking
dirt is on the floor, it's not
saying your thoughts out loud, I never
wanted to be an adult I never
saw adults laugh, it was always

looking up seeing degradation
and being told I'd put it there,
even when I couldn't reach,
they'd teach and tell me reasons why
like calculators can't be carried
on the hip, like otherwise

horrors would repeat, my phone
does long division, horrors
still repeat and adults make them happen,
still not laughing. Unless someone
says how they feel
or does something they love

that's real – I'm not real because I'm not an adult,
not even slightly real, I can't
imagine clean sheets a big deal, I can't
believe a sneer is better than a kiss
or that this and that
would only make me happy

if someone smaller were unhappy,
I still play with my food
and I make rude noises because it's funny,
I am still the smaller guy, I still cry
when told I caused the horror. This story's
short because I am never growing up.

New Bird

For Women that Write
(And Birds that Sing)

You be quiet when man is typing,
Qwerty tablets on their way
to rescue your titchy, smoking brow,
you are not now, nor will never be,
a wisdom pot as earthen-baked as he.

The postman came – he brought a list,
each point invented by the big game hunt,
your guide, more bold with each full colon,
he's grand before your pinafore
and more behaving like a... kindly sage.

Twice you've engaged your unsolicitor,
er, did you fucking stutter when you said
you wrote a book? So what? he wins
without the work, he can shirk and spin and spit.

This is your shit, your blushing wrong,
so knit yourself flat to the wall,
earwig well for his grand words
though he's never waited for his turn,
he reads his journal from the bush of fire,

and higher soars your scholarship,
your lip is trembling as he recites,
this night's his first
but he can execute most anything,
each side eye cannot ring amongst his bells,

well, he says, what do you think?
that's better isn't it, young miss? he never
kissed a page before but figured
since you did it, he could do it even more.

It's not his fault it falls,
crashing from the lofty nest
onto a clapless floor,
his Hamlin tune to all the cartoon clams,
they just don't understand a genius.

Woman, you write and you write the end,
you needn't even take a seat,
meekly applaud and believe his proclamation
that you'll never be as shined upon
as a man who always speaks.

Real Monsters

It's a Hollywood rule, if you're pretty you're dead,
if you drank or wore red,
the Count counts you up among 86 maids,
slits your tempting white throat, bakes you into a pie,
but don't die,
you taste so much better when you're live and afraid.

Swine before teens in the boulevard bar,
the haunt of the stars,
undaunted he glides in the neon pink lounge,
a grabbering phantom with trousers down
he will rip out your innards, try to turn you to mist
or you'll be on the shitlist.

Zombie zero will tell 'em now you would say no,
that you are the monsters,
whilst he's wiping the brains off his quadruple chin
and advances dead slow, groaning and rotten,
the automaton's queasy routine is a daily,
a saucer-eyed scream queen shut up in the box.

The Book of the Dead – you read your part,
has you tied down like Regan
with the Devil inside you, levitate from your mind,
head turned right round,
as he vows to cut your soul out and he's proud
to possess you or cast your first die.

In a VIP suite everyone hears you
Scream but your noise is a drop in the far distant
tide, frozen bride of the daemon, you hiss
fizz like a swan, vowing he and his makers
belong dead, in the mill, but yet still
you've the rabid saliva on windscreen and hood.

You're gonna need bigger lawyers, he gloats,
with his teeth, the relief when they drive verdicts straight
through his carcass we all play a role in the darkness
that cloaks him, and chokes at the starlets sacri-
ficed to his hell.
Crawling out of the well

they flung souls through the set,
poisoning apple with a million bucks bail,
you are not for sale, we utter, we raise,
as Ripley, as Carrie, as Starling, face morning, issue
a warning to all creatures that crawl, we say
freeze in the maze. Time's up. That is all.

The Presents

What did they say?
They said
and it's a very special day for her
cause today's her birthday!

But it isn't.
So I shake my head with smile, tiny frown
today's not my birthday
it's not for four months.

They look hurt for nine seconds then
grin and they say
Happy Birthday!
You only turn [inaudible mutter] once.

I haven't turned anything,
I'm still the same number,
I've still got the badge from last year,

They purse and severe,
say I'm a jolly good fellow,
Happy Birthday, my Dear!

I'm not jolly I say,
and they push me to space,
and wheel forth the icing on blazingest cake.

Let us cut you this piece —
biggest knife ever seen,
and the surface sinks-springs,

two different hands
on the big of my back,
Happy Birthday!

said back in the left ear and right,

and my shut lips have a slice
with a candle smeared on them, I don't

want to eat this,
I say into crumbs,
but they push it and force it
down onto my tongue,

have this on me,
tips a glass of parmaine,
you should celebrate today,
hangover schmangover,
down it, have a bottle, get it gone

it's a dead special day,
it's your birthday,
YOUR birthday!

But it's not,
it's a Tuesday
with bunting, balloons,

every double row teeth,
very western tradition,
each host with a song,

over over again,
dear name that's not mine,

and that's it for all time,
every day is my birthday,
whatever I say.

Mama Hen

Put it down, face up
so you can see the nose,
no clothes with signatures,
it grows, it grows,
My coins came up heads,
all pink line positive
and I became
the toaster oven bargain.

Don't tend the tears,
don't leave them screaming,
my father's teeth show in the beam,
and I miss the plus sign,
it was much more grateful
to be mine
songs repeat
till they turn to earth.

From each berth
I sailed unto
a one tree isle,
I'll never do this twice,
it's just too hard, too hard,
I'm no more starred out in midnight,
but staked out by a rocking chair,
a bear with one wet ear.

Pick it up, heat it up, mop it up,
sigh.
No swears but wears and tears
and don't you dares,
It's far too small to have a will,
but battled out, there is no out,
it's purple face
in each flash frame from now till close.

British Gaslight

Today, I saw myself from space,
I looked like I was falling down.

Me the ever people's land
complete with jagged beauty fringe,
natural, catching every kind,
but I'm not kind, you see.

They say to my hurt parts
that any kind is weaker yet,
tell me through their Eton mess
that yes, I am their very breath,
and bits of me believe.

I know, I know,
there have been signs,
they told me that I don't need friends,
so into bed now, take the meds,
I'm all but wed to plagued regime
if I don't get shot
I'm all but dead.

I brought it on myself, it's me
my national hist'ry and my sunk esteem
brings vani-me into their arms
and when they charm me,
call me Lion-heart and Always
there's less of me that tells them no.

They crow their love for my moon rivers,
grope my sun cities in their hand
but say my pits are way too deep,
my sleep is theirs to hang me with,
they rubbish all my wonder traits –
my sister-brother-parenthood,

my spectrum of colour and of sound,
the dancing facets of my crowds,
so I forget just who I am,

and wobble more and grip,
the chipped and faded souvenir mug,
de-united kingdom
and I'm married to a thug.

One side of my face screams
shut up behind the windows

so much of me knows that they are
death on the shelf,
but I don't deserve more, I'll never
have it so good,
who would love me with all my flaws?

They said I had remembered wrong
when I touched upon their pledge to care,
and when I showed the photo,
I was seeing what wasn't there.
And when their Auntie nods
and says they wouldn't lie,
who am I, just who am I?

I'm a country, a state
with a vulnerable side
I deserve to be cared about all of the time.
Not see my house burn down
and be advised it was I
who struck the match, I will
continue, I will catch,
I will drag backwards from the hedge funds
and come right back.

They have made me frightened for my place,
today, *today* I see myself from space.

It's not Me, it's You

Grinning an acorn chew
he tells me not to see that friend,
she's not a lily like me,
she rushes with the duvets.

Kissing me, he hides his gnash
in my own mouth, starts to graze
his hangnail on the bedpost
when it rains, he can't
open the window, I might
get the wrong idea.

He kneels above my chest with eyes
burning, beam from the height and slips
my breath from me,
standing on my
plait. Boa-ed in the cochlea, I'm
a rat with bulging eyes, he warns me
not to take a job, they won't
pay me like he does,
take the plane, be plain for me he says,
the one brown rodent
horned into his shoe. It's
not me – it's you.

He bangs my hand against the lamppost,
shows me cold, gold light in snow,
don't go, he yodels, hands free, fit.

Blonde, I go much fairer when he blows,
unreasonably slight, he stops and shares
his lemon twist, you're history
without me, Pearl. And then,

I'm not his girl.
I give my star-shaped friend a ring,

take a tender pool hall role,
breathe blondely at the streetlight. I
open my own window
and throw out all the blue, I will
certainly be history — it's
not me, it's you.

Our House to Raze

We translucent, see our distillation,
each drop of rule we spill into the cup,
look up and see eyeballs, clearest eyeballs,
twitching as you type.

Your type never learns, we earn your trust,
we earn your money, bag of ten,
we men, we drew a cancer in cement,
sat astride a blameless bench
all shaking head when heartache
is freeze-packed in wind,
your ink as acid
jogging in your mousy veins,
your place is cold outside.

We move forward toward, toward,
the germy nation, we encourage each sneeze,
drop screens and put them in the green bin, no such
thing… as liars any more… So long
go all the mighty whispers,
memorable lines, now it's shoving spittle
drunky ravings cradle any sore,
bewildered walk through years, your tears
are locked in registers, our fingers harder
still, that blue pill we made you swallow
keeps everything the same. Pray, what *is*
that sound outside?

This is the dawning of the crystal age,
we hereby make provision for fine
enabled clarity, we outlaw those darkening
ceilings, consign your envelopes to the grave.
But someone picked our peck
and waves it like an anthem,
now our bulls, they keep it
in a fist and burn the leaves on trees, we don't

claim to please you all,
we've set blazes on the neighbour's fence,
no sense in using eau to put it out,
outside, you call our names.

We wrote some burned ideas in mud,
black sticky tar along the pavement's edge,
you stick, you pick us every time,
and road blockades they tend to melt away.
We've got you in our groping hand,
the land is pulled out under you,
you may come near, your drum, your yell,
our bell to ring, your
singing baby children, you'll never
touch our gleam roulette, you'll never
get to know the wheel, kneel,
get back, go home, go blind. "Sir
they've got inside."

Tending

I am here, I am here
I'll be here every year

the masses are marrying greens with dry meats
and I counted the angel two scoops to the left
my breath too apparent over broken teeth plotting
that tarte au citron of a weathered December
remember, remember
which carpet is hers

I am here, I am here
I'll be here every year

No roses, no daffs and no leaves on the trees
just eighty bare arms making arches above
the merry outside all stuffed in their chairs
while the one who loved ribbons is present no longer
she is under the standing
demanding the grief

I am here, I am here
I'll be here every year

Today of all days when myth meets the mundane
my unwritten living is weightier still
hunched with her earth in my hands, and the stains
of the rain on her one note slate, I towered
above her tunnelled new home and I asked her
why she had dumped me
in five queasy pieces
and as ever she told me

I am here, I am here.
I'll be here every year

The Privilege

Has it been assumed I'm a Wendy or Joanne?
Have I needed to stand and explain that ain't my man
behind the black door?

Have I fulfilled a cream tea, clotted Cotswold fantasy,
O a Mama Bianco, singing Come on Eileen
pair of spoons at my knee?

Am I deemed underdone, face the colour of tripe,
a wetwipe, a white, a bland waxworking skin?
Through pink veneer

listen I listen I can't really hear.
Who tells me I must love my Angel Delight?
or at night I stand out

or got missed in the snow? Am I ordered to go
take back to the fjords my tinned mandarin smile?
Did anyone pile

all the praise like I'd won when Hathaway hadaway
with academy pals? Am I told all you Jim-Sals
look Alaistair Sim'lar his

twin sister headmistress, my milkness is all,
the fall I feel but I can walk away. Am I
urged to accept that

as representation, surely Clarkson's sufficient?
Were my family *pansticks* moving in opposite
were there sneers I'd stuff

artefacts into white vans, taking and naming
marbles where I can? have I seen *No discoloreds*
on the B&B pane, hear

don't notice your shade, I have loads of pale friends!
Light bulbs? White bulbs more like — oh it's only a joke!
and though I woke, my eyes

still are closed. Was I pressed to make up for Rose West?
advised for the best to keep hands up in schools?
Is it the rules

that I love the police, those PCs gone mad,
Is it said I must feel white inside, am I cut wide
find if I bleed

just the same, but fight back and be blamed for my visible
veins, my veins white as miss bunn the baker,
am I called traitor

if Norse isn't my myth was I told to wish
I should not be me? I see but I have so much
more to see.

The Stand

We only fight by standing firm,
we turn for only one,
he turns us on and makes us sail,
our pale and dancing arms he sends
straight up and we protest.

The night we cut with halting stance,
we stop you – who goes there?
we dare the stalk of dirty sway,
by day we count each breath
of our Sweetheart, east, north, west.

Our love, he calls us stars
and arms, we wave a greeting
when he rolls in with the tide,
white the peace, the paper lace
of doves and clean dawn sky.

Our winter strength, our dance
upon the hills we colour deeper
we keep him close, his widespread gasp,
the air the air! His fine wet hair
through waves and down the moors. We take it

more of music than of war,
and swing with our eternal wind,
in the bloodshot eye of power,
resistant string, he holds us,
but it's we that guard the isles.

We haunt the view from penthouse bow,
to us you show your backs but trust,
our union spilling light
all down your land, the revolution
starts with us, Stand, Silent Sisters, stand.